Winter

By Alex Jordan   Illustrated by David Sheldon

Target Skill Consonant Cc/k/
High-Frequency Words we, my, like

PEARSON

Scott
Foresman

Tap, tap, tap, tap.

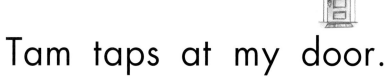

Tam taps at my door.

 Tam is cold.

Tam, have my cap.

 We pat, pat, pat at snowballs.

We tap, tap, tap at my snowman.

We like the snow.

Editorial Offices: Glenview, Illinois • Parsippany, New Jersey • New York, New York
Sales Offices: Needham, Massachusetts • Duluth, Georgia • Glenview, Illinois • Coppell, Texas •
Sacramento, California • Mesa, Arizona

Illustrations by David Sheldon

ISBN: 0-328-13062-1

8 9 10 V0G1 14 13 12 11 10 09 08

Kindergarten
Student Reader

Scott Foresman Reading K.2.4

PEARSON

Scott
Foresman

scottforesman.com

ISBN 0-328-13062-1

90000

9 780328 130627